Can I Have
Joy in
My Life?

The Crucial Questions Series
By R.C. Sproul

Who Is Jesus?

Can I Trust the Bible?

Does Prayer Change Things?

Can I Know God's Will?

How Should I Live in This World?

What Does It Mean to Be Born Again?

Can I Be Sure I'm Saved?

What Is Faith?

What Can I Do with My Guilt?

What Is the Trinity?

What Is Baptism?

Can I Have Joy in My Life?

Who Is the Holy Spirit?

Does God Control Everything?

How Can I Develop a Christian Conscience?

What Is the Lord's Supper?

What Is the Church?

What Is Repentance?

What Is the Relationship between Church and State?

Are These the Last Days?

CRUCIAL
QUESTIONS
No. | 12

Can I Have
Joy in
My Life?

R.C. Sproul

IR *Reformation Trust*   A DIVISION OF LIGONIER MINISTRIES, ORLANDO, FL

Can I Have Joy in My Life?

© 2012 by R. C. Sproul

Published by Reformation Trust Publishing
a division of Ligonier Ministries
421 Ligonier Court, Sanford, FL 32771
Ligonier.org   ReformationTrust.com

Printed in North Mankato, MN
Corporate Graphics
June 2016
First edition, seventh printing

Cover design: Gearbox Studios
Interior design and typeset: Katherine Lloyd, The DESK

All Scripture quotations are from *The Holy Bible, English Standard Version*®,
copyright © 2001 by Crossway Bibles, a publishing ministry of Good News
Publishers. Used by permission. All rights reserved.

Library of Congress Cataloging-in-Publication Data

Sproul, R. C. (Robert Charles), 1939-
  Can I have joy in my life? / R.C. Sproul.
    p. cm. -- (The crucial questions series; no. 12)
  Includes bibliographical references.
  ISBN 978-1-56769-295-2
  1. Joy--Religious aspects--Christianity. 2. Joy--Biblical teaching. I. Title.
BV4647.J68S67 2012
248.4--dc23

                              2012006008

Contents

Chapter One

DON'T WORRY,
BE JOYFUL

The word *joy* appears over and over again in the Scriptures. For instance, the Psalms are filled with references to joy. The psalmists write, "Weeping may tarry for the night, but joy comes with the morning" (Ps. 30:5b) and "Shout for joy to God, all the earth" (Ps. 66:1). Likewise, in the New Testament, we read that joy is a fruit of the Holy Spirit (Gal. 5:22), which means that it is a Christian virtue. Given this biblical emphasis, we need to understand what joy is and pursue it.

Sometimes we struggle to grasp the biblical view of joy because of the way it is defined and described in Western culture today. In particular, we often confuse joy with happiness. In the Beatitudes (Matt. 5:3–11), according to the traditional translations, Jesus said: "*Blessed* are the poor in spirit. . . . *Blessed* are those who mourn. . . . *Blessed* are the meek . . ." (vv. 3–5, emphasis added), and so on. Sometimes, however, translators adopt the modern vernacular and tell us Jesus said *happy* rather than *blessed*. I always cringe a little when I see that, not because I am opposed to happiness, but because the word *happy* in our culture has been sentimentalized and trivialized. As a result, it connotes a certain superficiality. For example, years ago, Charles M. Schulz, in the comic strip *Peanuts*, coined the adage, "Happiness is a warm puppy," and it became a maxim that articulated a sentimental, warm-and-fuzzy idea of happiness. Then there was the catchy song "Don't Worry, Be Happy," released by Bobby McFerrin in the 1980s. It suggested a carefree, cavalier attitude of delight.

However, the Greek word used in the Beatitudes is best translated as *blessed*, as it communicates not only the idea of happiness but also profound peace, comfort, stability, and great joy. So, we have to be careful when we come to the text of the New Testament that we do not read it through the lens of the popular understanding of happiness and thus lose the biblical concept of joy.

Think again about McFerrin's song. The lyrics are very odd from a contemporary perspective. When he sings, "Don't worry, be happy," he is issuing an imperative, a command: "Do not be anxious. Rather, be happy." He is setting forth a duty, not making a suggestion. However, we never think of happiness in this way. When we are unhappy, we think it is impossible to decide by an act of the will to change our feelings. We tend to think of happiness as something passive, something that happens to us and over which we have no control. It is involuntary. Yes, we desire it and want to experience it, but we are convinced that we cannot create it by an act of the will.

Oddly, McFerrin sounds very much like the New Testament when he commands his listeners to be happy. Over and over again in the pages of the New Testament, the idea of joy is communicated as an imperative, as an obligation. Based on the biblical teaching, I would go so far as to say that it is the Christian's duty, his moral obligation, to be joyful. That means that the failure of a Christian to be joyful is a sin, that unhappiness and a lack of joy are, in a certain way, manifestations of the flesh.

Of course, there are times when we are filled with sorrow. Jesus Himself was called "a man of sorrows, and acquainted with grief" (Isa. 53:3). The Scriptures tell us, "It is better to go to the house of mourning than to go to the house of feasting" (Eccl. 7:2a). Even in the Sermon on the Mount, Jesus said, "Blessed are those who mourn, for they shall be comforted" (Matt. 5:4). Given that the Bible tells us it is perfectly legitimate to experience mourning, sorrow, and grief, these feelings are not sinful.

However, I want you to see that Jesus' words could be translated as "Joyful are those who mourn." How could a person be in mourning and still be joyful? Well, I think we can unravel that knot fairly easily. The heart of the New Testament concept is this: a person can have biblical joy even when he is mourning, suffering, or undergoing difficult circumstances. This is because the person's mourning is directed toward one concern, but in that same moment, he possesses a measure of joy. I'll have more to say about this in the next chapter.

HOW CAN WE REJOICE ALWAYS?

In his letter to the Philippians, the Apostle Paul speaks about joy and about the Christian's duty to rejoice over and over again. For example, he writes, "Rejoice in the Lord always" (4:4a). This is one of those biblical imperatives, and it leaves no room for not rejoicing, for Paul says Christians are to rejoice always—not sometimes, periodically, or occasionally. He then adds, "Again I will say, Rejoice" (v. 4b). Paul wrote this epistle from prison, and in it he addresses very somber matters, such as the possibility that he will be martyred, poured out as a sacrifice (2:17). Yet he tells the Philippian believers that they should rejoice despite his circumstances.

That brings us back to this matter of how we can be joyful as a matter of discipline or of the will. How is it possible to remain joyful all the time? Paul gives us the key: "Rejoice *in the Lord* always" (emphasis added). The key to the Christian's joy is its source, which is the Lord. If Christ is in me and I am in Him, that relationship is not a sometimes experience. The Christian is always in the Lord and the Lord is always in the Christian, and that is always a reason for joy. Even if the Christian cannot rejoice in his circumstances, if he finds himself passing through pain, sorrow, or grief, he still can rejoice in Christ. We rejoice in the Lord, and since He never leaves us or forsakes us, we can rejoice always.

Since joy is a fruit of the Spirit, our sanctification is displayed not only by our love, peace, patience, kindness, and so forth, but by our joy (see Gal. 5:22–23). We must not forget that the fruit of the Holy Spirit is not the same as the gifts of the Holy Spirit. The New Testament shows us that the Holy Spirit distributes various gifts to various believers for various reasons. Not everyone has the gift of teaching. Not everyone has the gift of preaching. Not everyone has the gift of giving. Not everyone has the gift of administration. But when we come to the fruit of the Spirit, it is not as if some Christians have the fruit of faithfulness while others have love, or that some Christians have the fruit of goodness and gentleness while others have peace and self-control. Every Christian is to manifest all of the fruit of the Spirit, and the more we grow in grace, the further we progress in our sanctification, the more gentle we should be, the more patient we should be, the more faithful we should be, and, obviously, the more joyful we should be.

In simple terms, this means that the Christian life is not to be marked by dourness or a miserable attitude. We all have bad days, but the basic characteristic of a Christian personality is joy. Christians should be the most joyous people in the world because we have so much to be joyous about. That is why Paul does not hesitate to command his readers to rejoice.

THE WAY TO RECOVER JOY

Paul's admonition to believers to be joyful presupposes that believers can do something if they find themselves lacking in joy. He is right, of course, and the New Testament is filled with teaching on how to be joyful. The most basic method is to focus our attention on the ground of our joy, the source of our joy.

Paul gives one of the most practical of these teachings in Philippians: "Whatever is true, whatever is honorable, whatever is just, whatever is pure, whatever is lovely, whatever is commendable, if there is any excellence, if there is anything worthy of praise, think about these things" (4:8). This is a call to meditate upon the things of the Lord, to turn our attention to the things of God. When we find ourselves depressed, down, irritated, annoyed, or otherwise unhappy, we need to return to the source of our joy, and then we will see those circumstances that are sapping our joy in perspective. The circumstances of this life will pale into insignificance when compared to that which we have received from God.

Sometimes our joy is determined by the intensity of the latest blessing we experienced at the hands of God. We're always looking for the mountaintop experience, for a spiritual high that will excite us and fill us with joy, but these intense feelings wear off. When I have things in perspective, I know that if I never experienced another blessing in my entire life other than the blessings I already have received from the hand of God, I would have no possible reason to be anything but overflowing with joy until the day I die. God has already given me so much to be thankful for, so much to provoke my soul to delight, gladness, and joy, that I should be able to live on the basis of that surplus of blessedness and remain joyful all of my days.

Of course, the good news is that God will not stop manifesting His care and giving us His tender mercies and blessings. He continues to do that, and that means that every day we live as Christians we have more reason to rejoice than we had the day before. We have spent one more day receiving His love and all the benefits that He pours out on us, all those things that make us joyful.

What is the great enemy of joy? In the New Testament, it seems to be not so much sorrow or grief as anxiety. It is telling, I think, that immediately after commanding the Philippians to rejoice always, Paul goes on to say: "Do not be anxious about anything, but in everything by prayer and supplication with thanksgiving let your requests be made known to God. And the peace of God, which surpasses all understanding, will guard your hearts and your minds in Christ Jesus" (4:6–7). It almost seems as if Paul was an eye-witness to the Sermon on the Mount and heard Jesus say to His disciples: "Do not worry about your life, what you will eat or what you will drink; nor about your body, what you will put on. Is not life more than food and the body more than clothing?" (Matt. 6:25). It is anxiety that robs us of our joy. And what is anxiety but fear? Fear is the enemy of joy. It is hard to be joyful when we are afraid.

The prohibition that Jesus gave more than any other in all of His teaching was "Fear not." This, too, is an imperative, and again, the only solution is to go back to our Father. We need to go to Him in prayer, to fellowship with

Him. In this way, we stay close to the source of our joy. We shed our anxieties, and the fruit of the Spirit ripens in us again. If we understand who Christ is and what He has done for us, we have a new dimension of joy.

In the end, then, McFerrin's song is nearly on target. We should not worry, but we should be joyful.

Chapter Two

COUNTING IT ALL JOY

One of the hardest lessons we have to learn as Christians is to how to be joyful in the midst of pain and suffering. But joy in those circumstances is not optional. James tells us, "Count it all joy, my brothers, when you meet trials of various kinds" (1:2). What does James mean here, and how can we do what he commands us to do?

It is one thing to be in a state of joy and another thing

to count our circumstances as joyful. When James tells us to "*count* it all joy," he uses a word that carries the idea of reckoning, considering, or deeming. He is saying that even when we do not feel joyful about a trial we are enduring, we must count it—that is, consider it—as a matter of joy. We are to do this not because the thing we are enduring is pleasurable but because, as James says, "[we] know that the testing of [our] faith produces steadfastness" (v. 3). In other words, tribulation, pain, and suffering work patience within us, so something good happens to us even in the midst of trials. By remembering that truth, as we pass through trials, as difficult as they may be to bear, we will understand that they are not an exercise in futility, but that God has a purpose in them, and His purpose is always good.

My mentor, Dr. John Gerstner, made an interesting distinction between different kinds of bad and different kinds of good. Regarding things that are bad, he said there is "bad bad" and "good bad." Things that are "good bad" are, considered in and of themselves, destructive and painful—but they nevertheless can cause good. If this were not so, how could God have said through the Apostle Paul, "And we know that for those who love God all things work together for good, for those who are called according to his purpose" (Rom. 8:28)?

So, James is exhorting us to count it all joy even when it is not all joy, not because it is joyous to be involved in pain and suffering, but because God can bring good through that pain and suffering. He is working in even the difficult situations for our sanctification.

LOOKING TO THE BRIGHT FUTURE

In a sense, in order to be able to count earthly sorrows and afflictions as matters of joy, we have to cultivate the ability to think in terms of the future. Sometimes the Christian's hope of heaven is ridiculed as "pie in the sky." However, it is a reality that provides real comfort, as examples from history show.

In the days of slavery in the United States, there was very little for black slaves to be happy about. Their lives were filled with hardship and suffering. The labor of their hands was endless drudgery, day after day. They were often in want. Families were sometimes torn apart as individuals were sold. They lived a miserable existence, and yet, the music of the Negro spirituals from that time is full of joy. I do not think it is a coincidence that one of the chief recurring themes of those spirituals is heaven. For instance, in the spiritual "Swing Low, Sweet Chariot," one of the stanzas reads: "I looked over Jordan, and what did I see coming for to carry me home? A band of angels coming after me, coming for to carry me home." The powerful testimony of so many of these songs is that of a joy based on looking to God and future blessedness.

This way of looking at things is consistent with the New Testament. For instance, Paul acknowledges the reality and intensity of the pain we are called to endure in this world: "The Spirit himself bears witness with our spirit that we are children of God, and if children, then heirs—heirs of God and fellow heirs with Christ, *provided we suffer with him* in order that we may also be glorified with him" (Rom. 8:16–17, emphasis added). But then he makes a comparison between the afflictions we experience here and the joy that has been stored up for us in heaven: "For I consider that the sufferings of this present time are not worth comparing with the glory that is to be revealed to us" (v. 18). The temporal moments of anguish and suffering that we go through are as nothing compared with the joy that has been laid up for us in heaven.

However, heaven is still future, and the present is often

hard. Years ago, I had a friend, an elderly lady, who was marked by a buoyant spirit and an ebullient personality, and she kept those traits even when she was diagnosed with cancer. But one day when I visited her in the hospital as she was undergoing chemotherapy, I found her a little bit down. She wasn't her normal buoyant, cheerful self. I said, "Dora, how are you doing?" She looked at me with tears in her eyes and said, "R. C., it's hard to be a Christian with your head in the toilet." Then she laughed and the joy came back into her eyes. I laughed, too, because I could relate to what she was saying. When we are sick and in pain, it's hard to feel a lot of joy.

Paul's counsel, as we go through those periods, is to remember that God has put a time limit on our pain, and that after that time we will enter a condition wherein pain will be no more. There will be no more tears, no more pain, no more anxiety, no more sorrow, and no more adversity. That does sound like pie in the sky, but we cannot escape the fact that at the very heart of the Christian faith is the truth that this world is not our home. Our final destination still lies ahead.

So, heaven is the Christian's great hope, and the New Testament says hope is the anchor of the soul (Heb. 6:19).

Sadly, those who are without Christ are without this hope. I sometimes wonder, given how much I struggle with life as a Christian, how people who are not Christians make it. How do they endure without the hope of the joy that has been stored up for us in heaven? We should be much more thankful for this blessed hope than we are, and fix our eyes on the future in the midst of pain and affliction.

TRUSTING GOD THROUGH CALAMITIES

One biblical character who displays this outlook poignantly and graphically is the prophet Habakkuk. He was not particularly joyful when he saw his nation being ravaged by a foreign power. This situation created all kinds of theological difficulties for him; in a real sense, Habakkuk suffered a crisis of faith. He asked God: "How can You allow these things to happen? How can You let all this evil and suffering go on in this world? Aren't You too holy to even behold iniquity?" He said, "I will take my stand at my watchpost and station myself on the tower, and look out to see what [God] will say to me, and what I will answer concerning my complaint" (Hab. 2:1).

God responded to His mournful prophet by presenting

Himself to Habakkuk in a way that was quite similar to the way He came to Job. Afterward, Habakkuk said: "I hear, and my body trembles; my lips quiver at the sound; rottenness enters into my bones; my legs tremble beneath me. Yet I will quietly wait for the day of trouble to come upon people who invade us" (3:16). Habakkuk was overcome by the message of God to the point where his body shook.

The book of Habakkuk contains a short phrase that is quoted three times in the New Testament and serves as a thematic statement in the Apostle Paul's greatest theological work, the epistle to the Romans (Rom. 1:17). That phrase is, "the righteous shall live by . . . faith" (Hab. 2:4). It could be translated this way: "The righteous shall live by trust." What does it mean to live by faith other than to trust in God? The life of faith is not just about believing that God exists; it is about believing God or trusting God.

I have this conversation with myself every time I am afraid: "R. C., do you really trust God? Do you believe Him when He promises you that this is for good and for your ultimate joy?" Only if we believe God can we maintain joy in the midst of hardship.

How did Habakkuk respond to the Lord? He said: "Though the fig tree should not blossom, nor fruit be on the vines, the produce of the olive fail and the fields yield no food, the flock be cut off from the fold and there be no herd in the stalls, yet I will rejoice in the LORD; I will take joy in the God of my salvation" (3:17–18).

These words seem foreign to us because Habakkuk lived so long ago in a culture that was very different from ours. We never lose sleep at night worrying about the blossoming of figs. We do not worry about whether the olive crop will fail. But Habakkuk was a Jew, and Israel's economy was agricultural. Figs were an important commodity. So was the fruit of the vine, the grapes from which wine was made. One only needs to go to Napa Valley in California to see how important grapevines can be to a region's economy. If those grapevines are poisoned or destroyed by some kind of natural calamity, the whole region suffers economically. Likewise, in Habakkuk's day, olives yielded oil, which was very important in Israel. If people were not involved in vineyards, they were maintaining flocks. The livestock, too, was crucial.

Let me try to translate Habakkuk's words into modern terms: "Though the farming industry collapses, though the stock market crashes, though the automobile industry goes belly-up, though the technological industries explode, though all of these things happen, nevertheless, I will rejoice in the God of my salvation. I will joy in Him." That is what he would have said had he lived in the twenty-first century.

Habakkuk went on to say why he felt this way. "GOD, the Lord, is my strength; he makes my feet like the deer's; he makes me tread on my high places" (v. 19). A deer is so sure-footed, it can move like a mountain goat on high and dangerous places, crossing narrow ridges without falling to destruction. Habakkuk said that God would make his feet like the feet of a deer and cause him to walk on high places. He was saying that even though many calamities befell his people, though the nation was ravaged, though Israel was defeated in war, and though pestilence, disease, and crime affected everything, nevertheless, he would not be cast down into the valley, but God would make his feet like the feet of a deer, sure-footed, able to ascend into the high and holy places. God gives that kind of stability, even in the midst of calamity, to those who give their attention to Him and place their trust in Him. That's what Habakkuk meant when he said, "The righteous shall live by his faith." That's the basis for the joy that we have as Christians.

Chapter Three

How Do You Spell Joy?

All of us can remember moments or occasions when we experienced extraordinary joy, not only individually but also within our communities or even our nations. I can think of a couple of such episodes.

One day, when I was six years old, I was playing stickball in a street in Chicago. Home plate was a manhole cover right in the middle of the street, and in the center of that manhole cover was a small hole about an inch and a half in diameter. I remember that insignificant detail because my dad had bought me a slender little bat that I used to play stickball in the streets, and one day when it was my turn to hit, I dropped my bat and it somehow went down that hole and was lost forever. As you might imagine, that was not a joyous occasion, but another day when I happened to be at bat, right in the middle of the game, all heaven seemed to break loose around me. People started running out of the apartment buildings along the street, yelling, beating on dishpans with spoons, and generally acting in a crazy manner. Finally, I began to understand what everyone was yelling: "It's over; it's over." It was V-E Day, the day Nazi Germany surrendered to the Allies to end World War II in Europe. After a long and arduous struggle, that titanic conflict was over, and all the pent-up anxiety and pain of the people suddenly gave way to unspeakable joy, and they began celebrating. I had very little understanding of what all the fuss was about, but I certainly could tell that a lot of people were very happy. I just wished they had not interrupted my game.

A similar episode, not quite as dramatic, took place in 1960, when I was twenty-one years old. I had grown up in the city of Pittsburgh, which boasted a couple of professional sporting teams, the Pittsburgh Pirates and the Pittsburgh Steelers. The Steelers went for forty years before they won their first conference championship, much less a world championship. They were the perennial losers of the National Football League. However, their record was not as dismal as that of the Pirates. I followed every Pirates baseball game in the 1940s and 1950s. I practically lived at Forbes Field, and when I wasn't at the game, I was listening to it on the radio. I lived and died with the Pittsburgh Pirates, and we died a lot more often than we lived. They were the habitual cellar dwellers. We used to say that the Pittsburgh Pirates were in first place if you turned the newspaper upside down. So, we went through a lot of years of frustration—until 1960.

That year, the Pittsburgh Pirates actually won the National League pennant, and the state went crazy. But then, of course, they had to go to the World Series to face the mighty New York Yankees. No one thought the Pirates had any chance at all. In fact, the Yankees set the all-time record for the most runs scored in a seven-game World Series that year, but people don't remember that. What they do remember is that the Yankees *lost* the 1960 World Series to the Pittsburgh Pirates in one of the most dramatic moments in baseball history. In the seventh game of the World Series, the game was tied in the bottom of the ninth. The Pirates were batting, and I was there at Forbes Field, sitting along the third-base line. Bill Mazeroski, the Pirates' second baseman, was not a great hitter, but that day he slugged a home run to left center field, over the head of a dejected Yogi Berra. When that happened, pandemonium broke loose in Pittsburgh. When the ball cleared the fence, I jumped up and knocked down a little seventy-five-year-old lady. I said, "Oh, ma'am, I'm so sorry, I didn't mean to hurt you." She looked at me from the ground with a grin all over her face, and she said: "I don't care, Sonny, you could throw me all over the place. The Pirates have won their World Series." As I drove home from Forbes Field that day, I heard unceasing honking of car horns all over the city. There was great, great joy that day in Pittsburgh because of a baseball game.

ELATION AND DEJECTION

I have often wondered how a game can make people so happy—or so sad. As I mentioned, I lived and died with the Pirates when I was a boy. Later, when the Steelers became a powerhouse and began to win Super Bowls in the 1970s, it was the same. If the Steelers would lose a game, I would be depressed for a week and would have to remind myself, "It's just a game." This power of sporting events to leave us disappointed and down is captured well in the classic tale "Casey at the Bat" by Ernest Thayer. When Casey, the star of the Mudville baseball team, miraculously gets a chance to bat in the bottom of the ninth, the spectators assume he will hit a home run and win the game. What happens? Mighty Casey goes down swinging. Thayer ends the story with this stanza:

> Oh, somewhere in this favored land
> the sun is shining bright;
> the band is playing somewhere,
> and somewhere hearts are light;
> and somewhere men are laughing,
> and somewhere children shout;
> but there is no joy in Mudville—
> mighty Casey has struck out.[1]

---

1 From "Casey at the Bat" by Ernest Lawrence Thayer, 1888.

In high school, I played baseball, and we played for the city championship two years in a row. The first year, we won the championship in the final inning, and I will never forget that. I was so thrilled, I felt as if I was walking on air. The next year, however, we lost the championship game, and that was a terrible feeling. It's always that way when a championship is on the line. When the game is finally decided in favor of one of the teams, there is joy and wild celebration on the winning side. The players leap about, hug one another, and sometimes run up into the stands to rejoice with loved ones. Then the camera shifts to the losers' side, and there we see tears, dejection, and disappointment.

Of course, a game is not really *just* a game. The sports teams we cheer for and identify with vicariously represent not just our city or our nation, but each of us. They represent us in conflict, in competition, in striving for achievement. So many of the aspirations and hopes of human beings are expressed in things such as sporting events, which are really only representations of the human struggle. But have you noticed that when our team wins, we say, "*We* won," but when they lose, we say, "*They* lost"? We love to identify with a winner, but we are not happy to identify with a loser.

REJOICING EVEN IN LOSSES

After many years, I have begun to discover that it is possible for me to rejoice even when my team loses. How can that happen? It used to make me miserable to see the other team going through its celebrations after defeating my team. Finally, I began to see that those players were thrilled because they had achieved something they had worked so hard to accomplish. They were experiencing what was, for them, an occasion of great joy. It was not as if there had been a national disaster, in which everyone had suffered a loss. There was someone who was happy, and I began to find that I could take pleasure in their happiness.

After all, the Bible tells us, "Rejoice with those who rejoice, weep with those who weep" (Rom. 12:15). That is one of the key principles of joy. It teaches us that our joy is not to be restricted to our own circumstances or our own achievements, but that we ought to be able to feel joy for other people, for their achievements, for their successes, and for their bounty.

It has been said that every shot in the game of golf makes someone happy. If I hit a good shot, I'm happy but my opponent is unhappy. If my opponent hits a bad shot, it makes him unhappy but it makes me happy. But what does that say about me? It says my joy is too self-centered, so restricted to my own circumstances that unless things go the way I want them to go, the way in which I will directly benefit, I cannot be happy. To follow the New Testament ethic, I need to be able to rejoice with those who are rejoicing—and that includes those times when they are rejoicing because they have beaten me. The point is that we should not be jealous or covetous, but we should be able to enter other people's joy.

By the same token, we are called to enter other people's sorrow. This is what we call empathy, which involves feeling what others feel. Jesus Himself exemplified this virtue. How else can we explain the shortest verse in the Bible: "Jesus wept" (John 11:35)? Jesus, who proclaimed Himself to be "the resurrection and the life" (v. 25), came to the tomb of Lazarus knowing full well that He was going to raise His friend from the grave. But everyone there was mourning, including Lazarus' two sisters, Mary and Martha. They were Jesus' friends, so He entered their sorrow and wept with them as they wept.

It certainly takes grace to able to find joy in our hearts when people are experiencing joy over a gain that is, in some way, our loss. This involves more than just baseball games. It involves countless things that touch our daily lives. But God enables us as Christians to look at things not just from our own selfish perspectives but from the perspectives of others.

THE BEST WAY TO SPELL *JOY*

In the first year I was a Christian, I learned a simple acrostic with respect to the word *joy*. It taught that the letters that make up the word *joy* stand for "Jesus," "others," and "yourself," and the lesson was that the secret to joy is to put Jesus first, others second, and yourself third. Obviously that is a very easy idea, so simple that a young child can learn it and understand it, but it is far more difficult to get it into one's bloodstream. But this illustration contains a profound truth. Joy is often elusive because we put ourselves first and Jesus last. When that happens, we are trying to spell *joy* as y-o-j, and we need to rearrange our priorities.

Not only do we need to put Jesus first, we need to put others ahead of ourselves. I once had a lengthy conversation with a woman who was going through very difficult treatments for cancer. Through it all, however, she displayed a remarkable radiance. Every time I saw her, she seemed joyful. I began the conversation by asking, "How are you doing?" Well, she gave me a summary of how she was doing that lasted about fifteen seconds, then she said to me, "R. C., how are *you* doing?" I answered the question, but it was only after the conversation had ended and I was on my way that the truth came home to me. I had gone to her hospital room to comfort her and to manifest my concern for her well-being, but while we talked for about a half-hour, maybe fifteen seconds was devoted to her condition. For the whole rest of the time, we were talking about my troubles and worries, and she was comforting me. I couldn't believe it. It was no wonder she was so joyful; she was not wrapped up in herself in the least.

Jesus was called "a man of sorrows, and acquainted with grief" (Isa. 53:3), but He acquainted Himself with our sorrows and our griefs. Jesus is the only person in history who spelled the word *joy* without putting the letter "j" first. He put Himself last in order to make it possible for us to participate in joy. Still, even though Jesus was a man of sorrows, I believe He was the most joyful human being who ever lived, because He knew the Father better than any other human being. Also, He was more attuned to the will of God than any other human being and was utterly obedient to it, and obedience brings joy to the soul. Not even the pain and torment He had to endure was able to rob Him of joy.

So, if we would be joyful, we need to learn to rejoice with those who rejoice and weep with those who weep. But we cannot do that unless we somehow are able to escape from a life in which we care only about ourselves.

Chapter Four

THE GREATEST JOY

At one point during His earthly ministry, Jesus sent a group of His disciples out on their own to preach the gospel and to heal the sick and those who were under demonic possession. Luke writes:

> After this the Lord appointed seventy-two others and sent them on ahead of him, two by two, into every town and place where he himself was about to go. And he said to them, "The harvest is plentiful,

but the laborers are few. Therefore pray earnestly to the Lord of the harvest to send out laborers into his harvest. Go your way; behold, I am sending you out as lambs in the midst of wolves. Carry no money-bag, no knapsack, no sandals, and greet no one on the road. Whatever house you enter, first say, 'Peace be to this house!' And if a son of peace is there, your peace will rest upon him. But if not, it will return to you. And remain in the same house, eating and drinking what they provide, for the laborer deserves his wages. Do not go from house to house. When-ever you enter a town and they receive you, eat what is set before you. Heal the sick in it and say to them, 'The kingdom of God has come near to you.' But whenever you enter a town and they do not receive you, go into its streets and say, 'Even the dust of your town that clings to our feet we wipe off against you. Nevertheless know this, that the kingdom of God has come near.' I tell you, it will be more bear-able on that day for Sodom than for that town. Woe to you, Chorazin! Woe to you, Bethsaida! For if the mighty works done in you had been done in Tyre and Sidon, they would have repented long ago, sitting in sackcloth and ashes. But it will be more bearable in the judgment for Tyre and Sidon than for you." (10:1–14)

Jesus appointed seventy-two of His followers to go throughout the land of Palestine, to every hamlet and village where He Himself was about to go, to proclaim the coming of the kingdom of God. He warned them that in many places they would not be warmly received. As Jesus put it, they would be "lambs in the midst of wolves." Of course, the commission to go out with the message about Christ now belongs to all of the church, and so this warning applies to each one of us. The world is not always glad to receive our message, and sometimes we feel as lambs being led to the slaughter.

These must have been sobering words for the seventy-two. Luke does not explicitly say so, but I imagine they went out with a measure of trepidation. However, Luke is very explicit about the attitude of the seventy-two when they returned. He writes: "The seventy-two returned with joy, saying, 'Lord, even the demons are subject to us in your name!'" (v. 17). In all probability, they went out fearful and apprehensive, but they came back with exceedingly great joy. Why were they so happy? It was because they had been successful—God had used them and they had seen the manifestation of the power of Christ in their ministry. Also, they declared that they were happy because the demons were subject to them in Jesus' name. So, they were filled with elation because of two things—success and power. These are the kinds of things that we typically enjoy, too.

But Jesus did not quite enter into their joy. He told them: "I saw Satan fall like lightning from heaven. Behold, I have given you authority to tread on serpents and scorpions, and over all the power of the enemy, and nothing shall hurt you. Nevertheless, do not rejoice in this, that the spirits are subject to you, but rejoice that your names are written in heaven" (vv. 18–20).

We need to ponder these words. Jesus obviously understood the excitement of His followers, who had enjoyed the success of ministry, but He warned them against having a misplaced basis for their joy. He said they should not rejoice that the demons were subject to them; rather, they should rejoice that their names were written in heaven. Here our Lord identified the supreme foundation for Christian joy. Our joy is to come from the assurance that we have redemption in Christ. The greatest joy that a person can have is to know that his name is written in the Lamb's Book of Life, that he is saved and will live forever with Christ.

GUILT AND JOY

In the 1960s, I met a young man who had come to America from England less than a week before. His name was John Guest, and he went on to become an Episcopalian minister and national evangelist. When we first met in Philadelphia, he had hair down to his shoulders and a guitar strapped to his back; he looked very much like a member of the Beatles, and, in fact, he was from Liverpool, England, just as the Beatles were. John was working as an evangelist primarily on college campuses. He went to campuses with his rock band and sang to gather crowds, after which he preached and taught.

John's conversion had been something of a Damascus Road event. He went to a meeting where he heard the gospel, and his life was turned upside down. He met Christ and experienced the forgiveness of his sin. He shared with me that when he went home that night, he did not walk down the streets; rather, he skipped like a child, occasionally vaulting over fire hydrants. He was absolutely filled with joy in his new relationship to Christ.

I can relate to that. Knowing that one's sins are forgiven provides a tremendous relief. All of the burden of guilt is gone. Guilt is fundamentally a depressant. It squelches any feeling of well-being. It robs us of peace. It torments our souls. It is probably the most significant barrier to real joy. Thus, when our guilt is removed, joy floods our souls.

There is a difference between guilt and guilt feelings. Guilt is objective. Real guilt is incurred any time we violate or transgress the law of God. However, our feelings are not always in touch with reality. There are people in the criminal-justice system who are described as sociopaths or psychopaths because they can commit heinous crimes without feeling any remorse whatsoever. Still, their lack of feelings does not alter the reality of their guilt. Guilt is determined not by how we feel but by what we do. Nevertheless, there is often a close relationship between the objective and subjective dimensions of guilt—between the reality of the transgression itself and our subjective feelings of remorse and paralysis.

I see guilt feelings as being somewhat analogous to

physical pain. Pain is a symptom that something is objectively wrong in the body. Pain is a tremendous benefit to us medically, because it gives the signal that there is a problem that needs to be treated. Just as there are some people who feel no guilt for their crimes, there are people who have lost the capacity to feel things physically, and they are in grave danger every moment because they do not know when a serious illness has afflicted their bodies. The pain is the warning signal. So it is with guilt and guilt feelings. When I get a toothache, that tells me that something is wrong with my tooth. The pain drives me to the dentist to get my tooth fixed so the pain will stop. Guilt feelings should do the same thing; they should tell us something is wrong and motivate us to seek help. When our objective guilt is treated and the subjective guilt feelings go away, we feel great joy.

CONFUSING PLEASURE AND JOY

When I was a boy, my parents made me go to church every Sunday morning. I had no desire to go. I found the worship service boring and could not wait for it to be over so I could go play. But even worse than Sunday morning worship was the weekly catechism class, which was held on Saturday morning. That was the lowest point of my childhood experience in church. I had to go through a communicants class, then I moved on to the catechism class, where I and some other boys and girls had to memorize the Westminster Shorter Catechism. I endured it all just to become a member of the church and finish the course so my parents would be satisfied. I was not converted until several years later.

When I did become a Christian, I found myself wishing I had paid more attention in my catechism class. The only thing I remembered from the Shorter Catechism was the first question and answer, and the only reason I remembered that question was because I never could make sense out of it. The question was this: "What is the chief end of man?" The answer that we were required to learn and to recite was this: "Man's chief end is to glorify God, and to enjoy him forever." I just could not put those two things together. I understood, even as a child, that the idea of glorifying God had something to do with obeying Him, something to do with the pursuit of righteousness. But that was not what I was most singularly concerned about. It was not my chief end to be an obedient child of God by any means. And because it was not my chief end to be an obedient son to God, I could not understand how there was a relationship between glorifying God and enjoying Him. To me, the two seemed antithetical, incompatible.

My problem was that I was confused about two foundational ideas. I did not know the difference between pleasure and joy. What I wanted was pleasure, because I assumed that the only way I could have joy was by the acquisition of pleasure. But then I discovered that the more pleasure I acquired, the less joy I possessed, because I was seeking pleasure in things that required that I disobey God. That is the attraction of sin. We sin because it is pleasurable. The enticement of sin is that we think it will make us happy. We think it will give us joy and personal fulfillment. But it merely gives us guilt, which undermines and destroys authentic joy.

My conversion was fundamentally an experience of the forgiveness of God. If there had been a fire hydrant where I was when I was saved, I would have jumped over it, because I experienced the difference between pleasure and joy. I discovered in my own conversion the same thing John Guest discovered.

Psalm 51 is the greatest example of repentance that we

find anywhere in Scripture. In this psalm, David, under the conviction of the Holy Spirit, is brought to repentance for his sin with and against Bathsheba. He is broken and contrite in his heart, and he comes before God and begs for forgiveness. He says, "Restore to me the joy of your salvation" (v. 12a). Those who have experienced the forgiveness of God and the initial joy of it always need to have that joy restored, to have the guilt of their continuing sin removed so joy may return. As we seek forgiveness from God on a day-to-day basis, we return to the beginning of our joy—the day we discovered that our names are written in heaven.

Untold billions of people have never experienced the joy of salvation. If you are one of them, I say to you that there is nothing like it in the world. Just imagine having every sin that you have ever committed erased by God, having all of the guilt you have accumulated and the attendant feelings of guilt removed. That's what Christ came to do. He wants to give us joy, not power or success. His gift is the joy that comes from knowing that our names are written in heaven.

Chapter Five

FULLNESS OF JOY

One of the unique features of John's Gospel that has been a delight for Christians through the ages is the famous "I am" sayings of Jesus. For example, Jesus said, "I am the bread of life" (6:48); "I am the light of the world" (8:12); "I am the door" (10:7); "I am the good shepherd" (10:14); and "I am the resurrection and the life" (11:25). All of these statements help us better understand who Jesus is and what He accomplished for His people during His earthly sojourn.

In all of the biblical accounts of Jesus' "I am" statements, the Greek has a strange form. Usually, "I am" is the translation of the Greek word *eimi*. But in Jesus' "I am" sayings, the Greek is in an intensive form: *ego eimi*. It's almost as if Jesus is stuttering, as if He were saying, "I, I am."

It is fascinating to me that this particular Greek phrase, *ego eimi*, is used in the Septuagint, the Greek translation of the Old Testament, to render the Tetragrammaton, the great name of God: "I AM WHO I AM" (Ex. 3:14), which is usually rendered as *Yahweh* in the Hebrew. When *Yahweh* was translated into Greek, the translators used the phrase *ego eimi*. Thus, it seems that Jesus was consciously identifying Himself as God through His "I am" statements.

The last of the "I am" sayings in John's Gospel appears in the fifteenth chapter, where John tells us that Jesus said, "I am the true vine, and my Father is the vinedresser" (v. 1). Note that Jesus did not simply say He is the vine; He specified which vine He is—the *true* vine, which means He is the genuine vine or the authentic vine. Why did He make this distinction? He did not say, but there is an explanation that is accepted by most biblical scholars. They note that in the Old Testament, God entered a particular and special relationship with His people, the nation of Israel, and thereafter they are regularly depicted as God's vine or God's vineyard (Isa. 5:7; Hos. 10:1). Israel is the vineyard that God planted, nurtured, pruned, and used for the purpose of producing fruit that would nourish and enrich the whole world.

In the New Testament, we discover that Jesus came not only to redeem His people but also to embody the nation of Israel itself. In an ultimate sense, Jesus is the Israel of God. For instance, God said through the prophet Hosea, "When Israel was a child, I loved him, and out of Egypt I called my son" (11:1). Israel, the nation that God redeemed from slavery in Egypt, was called the son of God. Shortly after Jesus was born, an angel warned Joseph to flee to Egypt to escape from the jealous King Herod. Later, when the family returned to Israel, Matthew cites this verse from Hosea in reference to Jesus: "This was to fulfill what the Lord had spoken by the prophet, 'Out of Egypt I called my son'" (Matt. 2:15). So, we see this metaphorical identity or connection between the nation of Israel and Jesus. Jesus had a kind of solidarity with the historical people of God.

That idea was partially communicated when He said, "I am the true vine." However, He was also saying that Israel had failed to enrich the world as the vineyard of God.

Because of that, Jesus appeared as the true vine, with His Father as the vinedresser, the One who plants the vine, cultivates it, and prunes it.

LIFE THROUGH THE VINE

Jesus continued, saying, "Every branch in me that does not bear fruit he takes away, and every branch that does bear fruit he prunes, that it may bear more fruit" (v. 2). I do not have a green thumb and my knowledge of horticulture is very rudimentary. However, I have experimented with growing roses, and I have learned that after the blossoms begin to decay, they have to be cut off at a certain point on the stem. If I am diligent in pruning away the dead aspects of the bush, the blossoms become even more brilliant in time. This process seems counterintuitive to me; I would assume that by cutting off part of a bush I would be harming it or even destroying it. But the pruning process focuses the nutrients in the bush, causing it to bear fruit more consistently. This process is especially important in the tending of grapevines, which is the vine that is in view in Jesus' metaphor.

Going on, Jesus said, "Already you are clean because

of the word that I have spoken to you" (v. 3). Here He addressed Himself to His disciples, to believers, to those who already enjoyed fellowship with Him and had a saving relationship with Him. They were already "clean," He said. Then He added: "Abide in me, and I in you. As the branch cannot bear fruit by itself, unless it abides in the vine, neither can you, unless you abide in me" (v. 4).

What happens to the branches that are pruned from a tree or bush? After they are cut off, they wither and die. They are cut off from their life supply. Obviously such dead branches will not produce any fruit. They are impotent.

One day, during a cookout at the home of one of his members, a minister wandered over to the grill to speak to the host, who had stopped attending the weekly worship services. The minister was hoping to encourage him to begin attending once more. When the minister asked the man why he had stopped coming, the man replied: "I'm a Christian, but I don't feel that I need the church. I can do very well on my own. I'm an independent type of person. I don't need the fellowship of other people to boost me in my walk with the Lord."

While the minister listened to the man's explanations, he noticed that the charcoal on the grill was glowing white hot. Without saying anything, the minister picked up a set of tongs and moved one of the glowing coals apart from the others. He then continued his conversation with the parishioner. However, after a few minutes, he reached into the grill and picked up the coal with his bare hand. He then looked at the man and said: "Did you see what just happened here? Only a few minutes ago, I wouldn't have dared to touch this coal because it was so hot. But once I separated it from the rest of the coals, it stopped burning and became cold. It no longer could help cook the steaks on the grill. That is what is going to happen to you. You need the body of Christ. You need the church of Christ. You need the fellowship of the saints and the assembly of the people of God. We are not rugged individualists who are called to live in isolation from others."

That minister was right. The company of other believers keeps our faith lively and active. But if we cool off when we are removed from connection with other Christians, how much more will we wither if we remove ourselves from the real source of power, which is Christ Himself?

That is the point Jesus was making here. We will be fruitless and will wither spiritually if we do not abide in Christ, the true vine. The Greek word translated as "abide" here is *meno*. It also can be translated as "remain" or "stay." If we want to be productive, we cannot simply visit Jesus every now and then. We need to abide in Him.

Let me stress that Jesus was not speaking here about losing one's salvation. That is another matter. But He was reminding us that we are prone to wander, to cease to tap into the source of our power and our spiritual vitality, which is Christ Himself. So, His lesson for us is to stay close: "Abide in me, and I in you. As the branch cannot bear fruit by itself, unless it abides in the vine, neither can you, unless you abide in me." Simply put, all of the efforts that we make to be joyful, to be productive, or to achieve anything worthwhile in the kingdom of God are exercises in futility if we try to do them by our own power. Christians need to understand that without a strong connection to Christ, who is the power supply, we will be completely fruitless.

FULLNESS OF JOY

Jesus continued, saying:

> "I am the vine; you are the branches. Whoever abides
> in me and I in him, he it is that bears much fruit, for

apart from me you can do nothing. If anyone does not abide in me he is thrown away like a branch and withers; and the branches are gathered, thrown into the fire, and burned. If you abide in me, and my words abide in you, ask whatever you wish, and it will be done for you. By this my Father is glorified, that you bear much fruit and so prove to be my disciples. As the Father has loved me, so have I loved you. Abide in my love. If you keep my commandments, you will abide in my love, just as I have kept my Father's commandments and abide in his love. These things I have spoken to you, that my joy may be in you, and that your joy may be full." (vv. 5–11)

It was only in the final verse of this passage that Jesus explained why He had taught the disciples these things: "that my joy may be in you and that your joy may be full." Notice three things in this important teaching.

First, the joy that Jesus wants to see in us is *His* joy. Earlier, Jesus spoke to His disciples about peace, saying, "Peace I leave with you; my peace I give to you. Not as the world gives do I give to you" (John 14:27). Where does the Christian's peace come from? It comes from Him; in fact, it is His peace. In like manner, His own joy is available to us, and He wants to see it abiding in us.

Second, He wants His joy to *remain* in us. He wants us to have a permanent joy, not a roller-coaster ride of moods shifting between joy and misery. If we want to be consistently joyful, we need to abide in Him.

Third, He distinguishes between His joy and our joy, and expresses the desire that our joy should be full: "And that your joy may be full." Isn't that what we want? We do not want a partial cup of the fruit of the Spirit. We do not want just a little bit of joy. We want all of the joy that the Father has stored up for His people. That fullness of joy comes from Christ. It is first His joy that He gives to us, and as we are plugged into Him, this joy that comes from Him grows, increases, and becomes full.

No one who is reading this booklet has ever experienced the highest level of joy that is available to the people of God. However much joy you have at this moment, there is more joy to be had. There is a fullness that awaits us as the fruit of the Spirit is nurtured by the true vine.

About the Author

Dr. R.C. Sproul is the founder and chairman of Ligonier Ministries, an international multimedia ministry based in Sanford, Florida. He also serves as copastor at Saint Andrew's, a Reformed congregation in Sanford, and as chancellor of Reformation Bible College, and his teaching can be heard around the world on the daily radio program *Renewing Your Mind*.

During his distinguished academic career, Dr. Sproul helped train men for the ministry as a professor at several theological seminaries.

He is the author of more than ninety books, including *The Holiness of God*, *Chosen by God*, *The Invisible Hand*, *Faith Alone*, *Everyone's a Theologian*, *Truths We Confess*, *The Truth of the Cross*, and *The Prayer of the Lord*. He also served as general editor of *The Reformation Study Bible* and has written several children's books, including *The Donkey Who Carried a King*.

Dr. Sproul and his wife, Vesta, make their home in Sanford, Florida.